BEGINNING BLUES GUITAR MASTERY

ROCKLIKETHEPROS
© 2021 TERRY CARTER

ISBN-13: **9-781735-969244**
ROCKLIKETHEPROS.COM
© 2021 TERRY CARTER

TABLE OF CONTENTS

BEGINNING BLUES GUITAR MASTERY - INTRO	01
HISTORY OF THE BLUES	03
01 - **BLUES FORM**	04
02 - **STRAIGHT VS SWING - 1/8th NOTES**	05
03 - **HOW TO HOLD A PICK**	06
04 - **WALKING THE BLUES**	07
05 - **GETTING STARTED WITH THE BLUES**	08
06 - **BLUES SHUFFLE IN A** - VARIATION **#1**	09
07 - **MINOR PENTATONIC / BLUES SCALE**	10
08 - **RIVER BLUES SOLO**	11
09 - **STRUMMING BLUES IN A**	13
10 - **FINGERSTYLE BLUES** - COUNTRY STROLLING	14
11 - **BLUES SHUFFLE IN A** - VARIATION **#2**	15
12 - **GOLD RUSH BLUES SOLO**	16
13 - **OCTAVE JUMP BLUES IN A**	17
14 - **BLUES SHUFFLE IN A** - VARIATION **#3**	28
15 - **GREASY BLUES IN E**	19
TERRY CARTER's MESSAGE FOR YOU	21
THE ESSENTIALS	A
HOW TO READ TAB	B
GUITAR PARTS	C
GUITAR HANDS	D
NOTES ON THE GUITAR NECK	E
UNDERSTANDING CHORD DIAGRAMS	F
MUSIC SYMBOLS TO KNOW	G
GUITAR CHORD CHART	I
BASIC RHYTHMS	K
ESSENTIAL RHYTHMS	L
ABOUT THE AUTHOR	M
ABOUT TERRY CARTER MUSIC STORE	N
ABOUT ROCK LIKE THE PROS TEACHING SITE	O

BEGINNING BLUES GUITAR MASTERY

Welcome to the Beginning Guitar Blues Mastery book by Rock Like The Pros and written by Terry Carter. This is the most comprehensive beginning Blues guitar book in the world. In the Beginning Guitar Blues Mastery book, you are going to dive deep into learning and understanding all styles of Blues rhythm, Blues fingerstyle, and Blues soloing on the guitar.

In this book you are going to explore all the techniques and tools that you need to become a Guitar Blues Master. You are going to learn Blues Shuffle, Walking Blues, Blues Rock, Fingerstyle Blues, Boogie Woogie Blues, Jump Blues, Country Blues, Blues Scales, and Blues Soloing.

The Rock Like The Pros Beginning Blues Guitar Mastery book is a step-by-step introduction to the Blues, which means each lesson will build upon the last, so that you develop the proper feel and confidence you need to become a Blues Master.

One of the key concepts in this book is understanding the difference between Swing and Straight Feel. This is extremely important to not only understand the differences, but to be able to execute flawlessly, the two styles. Blues Swing is the primary style you hear in the Blues Shuffle, Boogie Woogie, Jazz Blues, and Slow Blues. Straight Blues is a faster, more driving style that you'll hear in Blues Rock (like Chuck Berry), Jump Blues, and Country Blues. Don't worry if you don't understand this concept right now; you will by the time you are done with the Beginning Guitar Blues Mastery book by Terry Carter.

Not only will the Beginning Blues Guitar Mastery book help you understand the different styles of Blues rhythm, it will teach you how to play a Blues solo. That's right, you are going to learn the holy grail of being a Blues master, which is the ability to solo over a Blues. Don't worry if you have never soloed before, this book will show you how to take the most popular scales used in Blues, the Minor Pentatonic and the Blues Scale, and use them to solo. When you are done with this book, you will turn heads as you learn the licks and riffs that have been used by all the Blues greats.

The Beginning Guitar Blues Mastery book is the most comprehensive book on Guitar and is written by Terry Carter, the leader in the Guitar world. Terry spent over

20 years as a Los Angeles studio musician, producer, and writer, working with greats such as Weezer, Josh Groban, Robby Krieger (The Doors), 2-time Grammy winning composer Christopher Tin (Calling All Dawns), Duff McKagan (Guns N' Roses), Grammy winning producer Charles Goodan (Santana/Rolling Stones), and the Los Angeles Philharmonic.

Terry has written and produced tracks for commercials (Discount Tire and Puma) and TV shows, including Scorpion (CBS), Pit Bulls & Parolees (Animal Planet), Trippin', Wildboyz, and The Real World (MTV). He has self-published over 10 books for Rock Like The Pros and Uke Like The Pros, filmed over 30 guitar and ukulele online courses, and has over 125,000 subscribers on his Rock Like The Pros and Uke Like The Pros social media channels. Terry received a Master of Music in Studio/Jazz Guitar Performance from University of Southern California, and a Bachelor of Music from San Diego State University, with an emphases in Jazz Studies and Music Education. He has taught at the University of Southern California, San Diego State University, Santa Monica College, Miracosta College, and Los Angeles Trade Tech College.

Whether you are a beginner at the Blues, or a seasoned veteran, the Beginning Guitar Blues Mastery book is going to take you deep into the world of the Blues, and you will come out a better, more confident guitar player, who will be ready to tackle the world. Are you ready? Let's dive in.

Sounds Good?
It's now your turn to dive into the *Blues Guitar Mastery!*

HISTORY OF THE BLUES

The Blues has a long history as an American artform dating back to the mid-1800's. The Blues was created out of African Spirituals that were born out of work songs or field songs. These songs were sung not only out of tradition, but to also help pass the time, and became the basis of the Blues that we know today. There are 3 key parts you want to remember about the Blues:

1. Call & Response
This is the where one person or group would sing a phrase and then another person or group would respond to that phrase.

2. 12 Bar Blues Form
The 12 Bar Blues is the most common form for all Blues. Although some Blues can be 8 or even 16 bars long, the majority are 12 bars. This is a form you want to get down into your soul, so you know exactly where you are in the form of the 12 Bar Blues at any time.

3. Blues Scale
The main scale that is used to create Blues melodies, and to solo, comes from the notes of the Blues Scale. The Blues Scale is the same as the Minor Pentatonic Scale except that it has an added "Blue Note" in it (the b5 Note).

a. For example:
i. CALL – "When He Walks In The Joint"   ii. RESPONSE – "Everybody Turns To Look"

b. Call & Response can also happen between the voice and an instrument. B.B. King is famous for this, as he would sing a phrase (Call) and then answer it with his guitar (Response).

The Blues Scale in A would be: **A - C - D - Eb - E - G - A**

BLUES FORM

The Blues form consist of 12 bars that alternate between the I, IV, and V chords (usually seventh chords) of the key you are in. The Blues shown below is a 12 bar Blues in the key of "A" Major or simply called "Blues in A." Bars 1-4 are played on the I chord, in this case A7, bars 5-6 are played on the IV chord or D7, and bars 7-8 return to the I chord or A7. Bar 9 is played on the V chord or E7, and bar 10 is played on the IV chord or D7. The last 2 bars (11-12) are called The Turnaround. Bar 11 returns to the I chord or A7 and bar 12 goes to the V chord or E7 before the entire 12 bars repeat or it ends on the A7 chord.

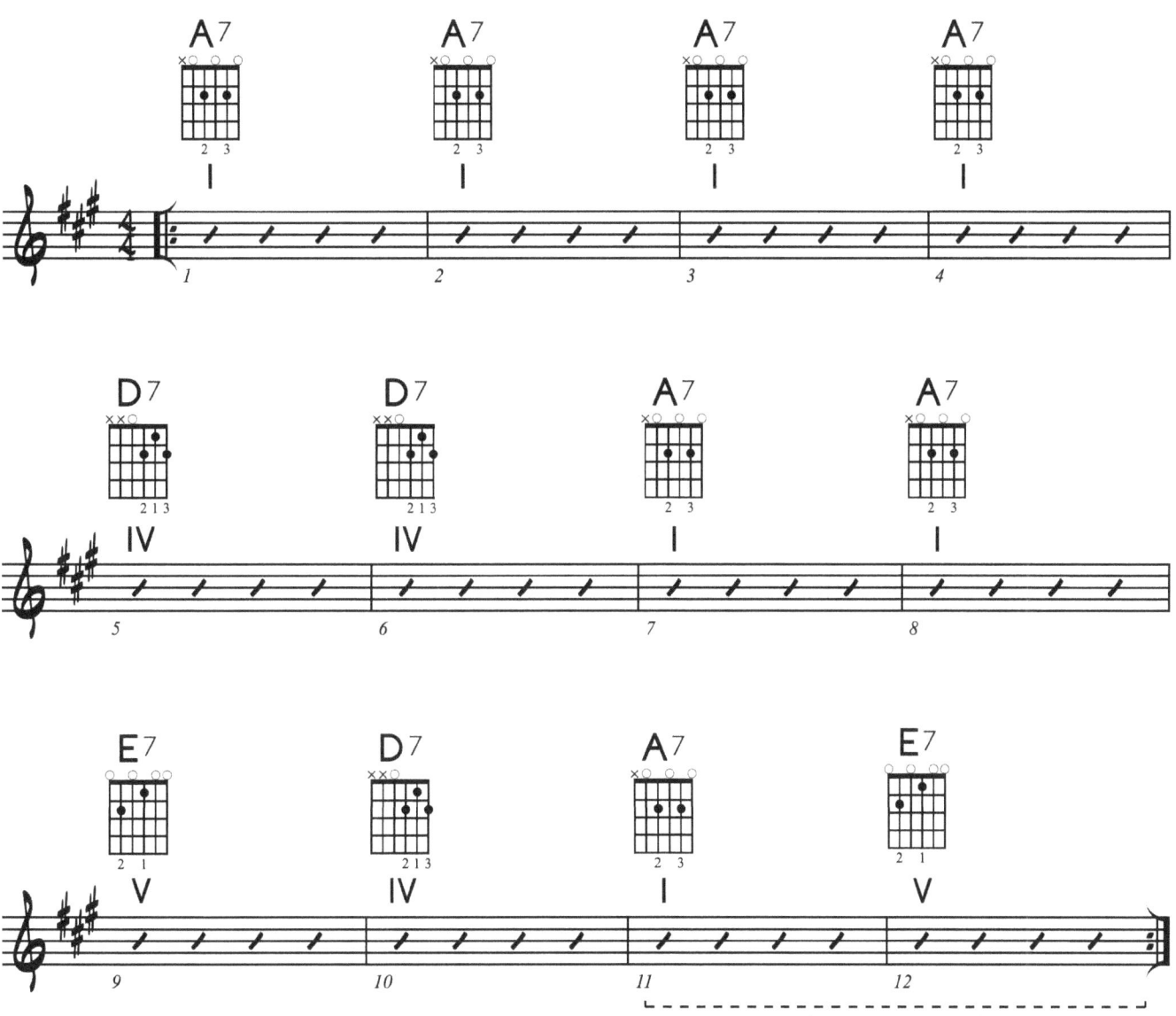

STRAIGHT VS SWING 1/8th NOTES

As a Blues Master it is absolutely necessary to be able to switch between playing swing 1/8th notes and straight 1/8 notes.

Straight 1/8th notes are the easiest because all you have to do is divide the quarter note beat into 2 equal parts and count them 1 + 2 + 3 + 4 +. You'll hear straight 1/8th notes in Blues Rock, Country Blues, and Jump Blues.

Swing 1/8th notes are a little harder to play and many times you'll hear people say, "just feel it." Although playing swing 1/8th notes is a feeling, you must understand how to divide the beat and play them properly. Let's start with a triplet, which is 3 notes per beat, and counted 1-trip-let, 2 trip-let, 3 trip-let, 4 trip-let.

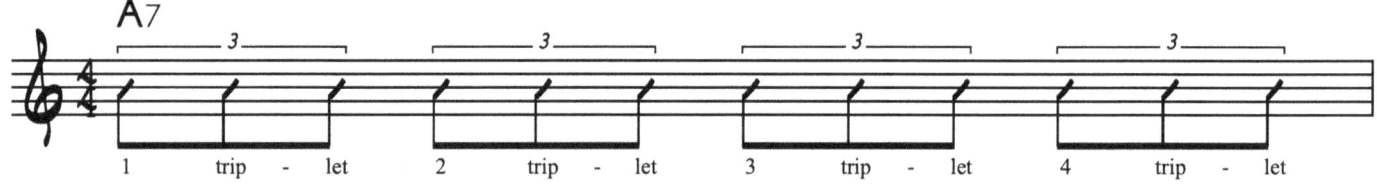

Now that you have mastered the triplets, to play Swing 1/8th notes simply play the first and the third note of each triplet, or don't play the middle note of the triplet "trip."

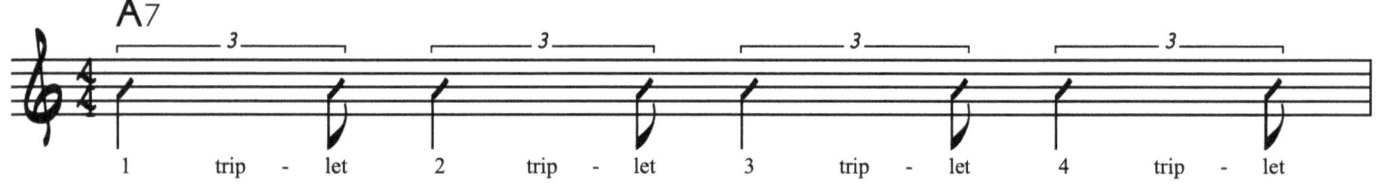

You'll hear Swing 1/8th notes in Blues Shuffle, Boogie Woogie, Jazz Blues, and Slow Blues.

HOW TO HOLD A PICK

Playing with a pick is one of the main ways to play the guitar. There are many different types of picks out there, made of different materials, thicknesses, and shapes. There is no right or wrong pick, it's simply the pick that feels comfortable and sounds pleasing to your style.
A good place to start is a Rock Like The Pros pick, available at **terrycartermusicstore.com**.

To hold the pick, grip it between your thumb and index finger. You need to grip it tight enough so that it doesn't slide around when you play, but not so tight that you are feeling strain in your fingers or wrists. A good place to strum the guitar is halfway between the end of the fretboard and the bridge. Most likely this will be towards the bottom of the soundhole.

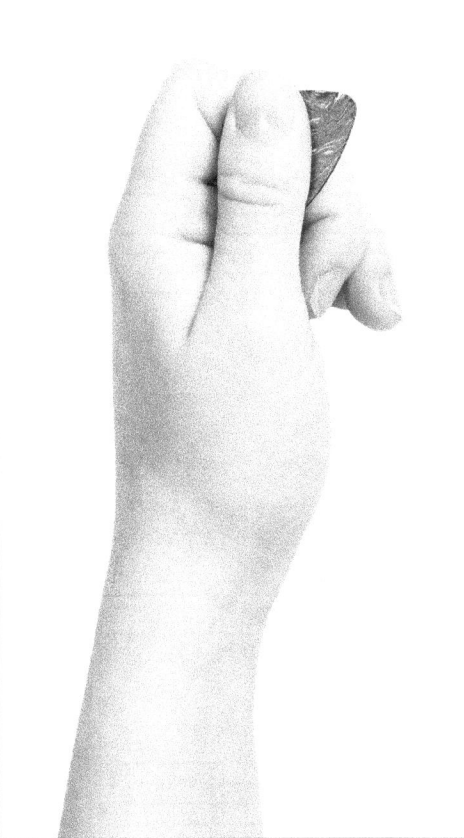 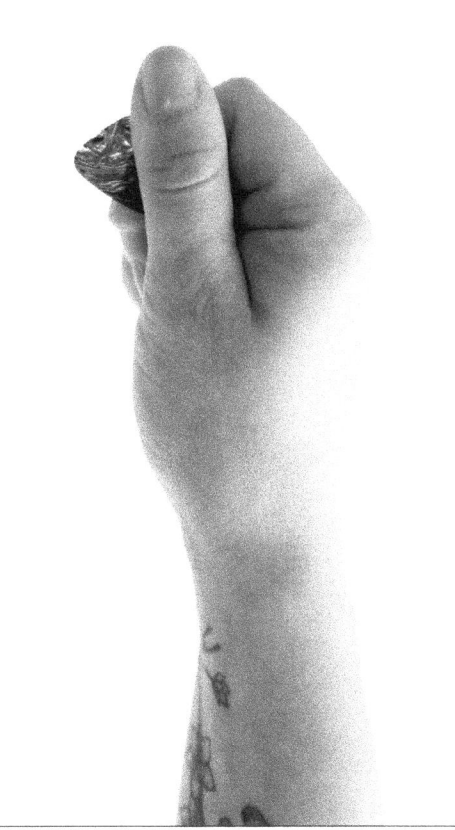 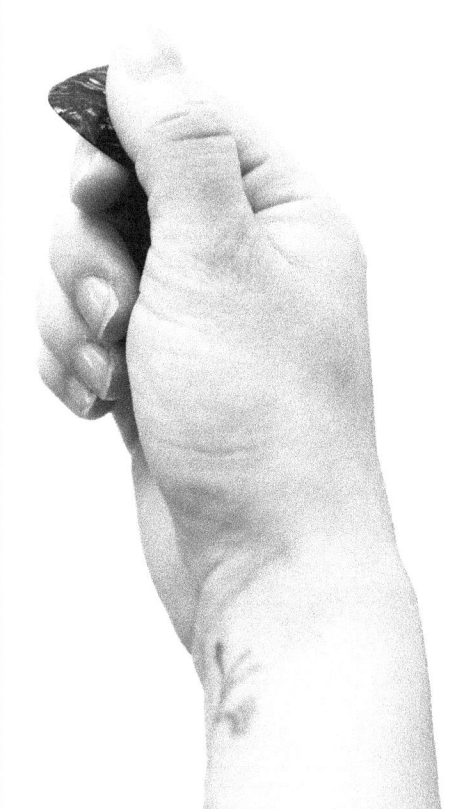

WALKING THE BLUES

In this introduction to the Blues lesson you are going to play all single notes. The great thing about this lesson is that every phrase is identical but played on a different string. The A7 phrase is played on the 5th string, the D7 on the 4th string, and the E7 on the 6th string. Play this with a swing 1/8th notes. Start by using all downstrokes and then try alternate picking (down, up, down up, etc...). The Sim. stands for simile and means to continue playing the previous pattern.

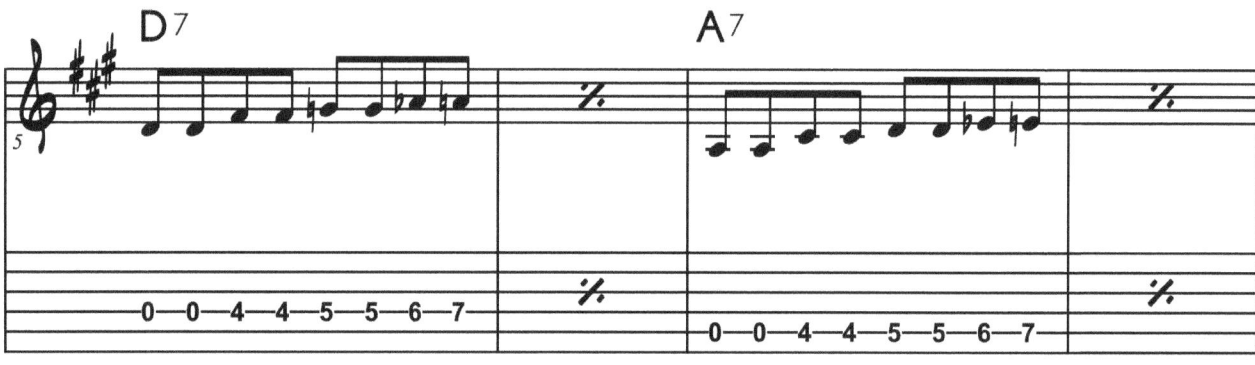

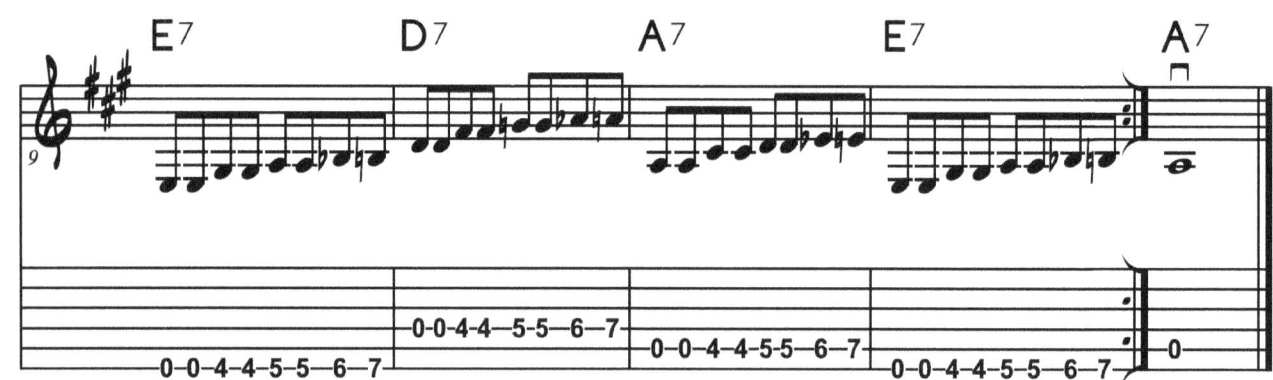

GETTING STARTED WITH THE BLUES

Welcome to the Blues!!! This lesson will help you get started playing a Standard Blues Shuffle, one of the most widely played styles in Blues. The first 4 bars will help you get used to playing two strings at the same time and then the last 4 bars will add some movement to give you that Traditional Blues Shuffle sound. Be sure to use all downstrokes and play both strings with equal force. Common mistakes are playing only the 5th or 4th string by themselves or accidentally hitting the 6th string.

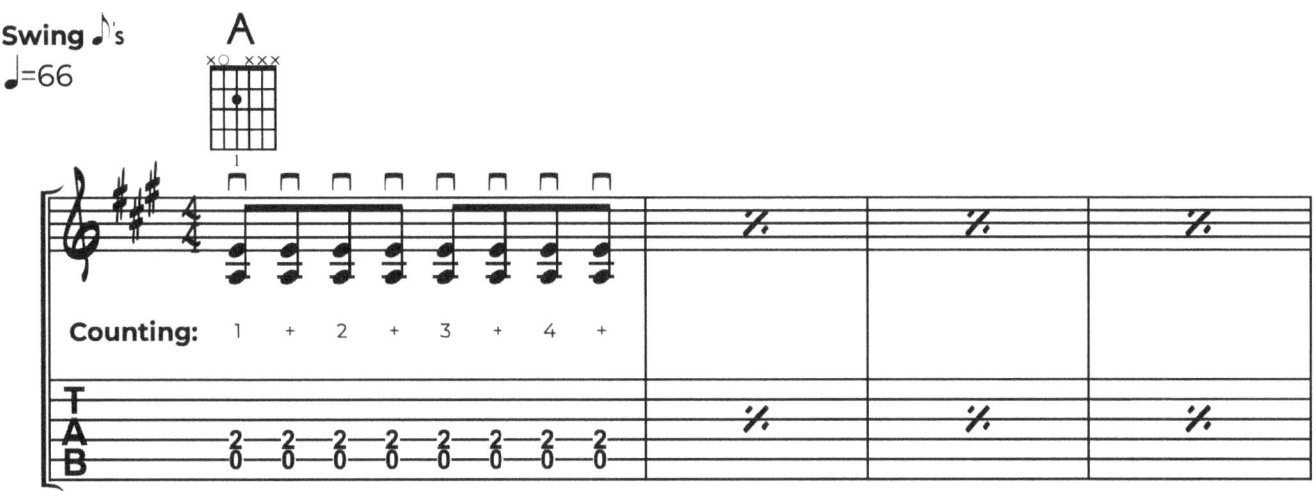

ROCKLIKETHEPROS.COM

BLUES SHUFFLE IN A VARIATION #1

This is the most important Blues rhythm lesson you need to know. This variation #1 is just the beginning to opening up the world of Blues Shuffle to your playing. This will just use the same 2 string Shuffle pattern as our previous lesson, but will take it through the 12-bar progression using the I (A7), IV (D7), and V (E7) chords. The last 4 bars are the most difficult to play because you are switching strings every measure.

The Turnaround

MINOR PENTATONIC & BLUES SCALE

The minor pentatonic and the Blues scales are the most widely used scales for all styles of music, especially Blues, Rock, Funk, and Jazz. It is very important to memorize these scales using the proper fingerings. These scales are used regularly when guitarists begin to improvise or play a solo. Start by using all downstrokes and then use alternate picking, down, up, down, up, etc...

"A" Minor Pentatonic: This scale is called the "A" Minor Pentatonic because the first note you play is an "A" on the fretboard.

"A" Blues Scale: This scale is similar to the Minor Pentatonic except that it adds an extra note to the scale giving it a bit more of a "bluesy" sound.

RIVER BLUES SOLO

This Blues solo sounds great over the Blues Shuffle in "A" and all the notes come right from the "A" Minor Pentatonic Scale. The easiest way to think of this solo is that it is taking small fragments from the Minor Pentatonic scale, called "licks," and creating a cool and cohesive sounding solo. There is a lot of repetition and each lick starts on beat 2.

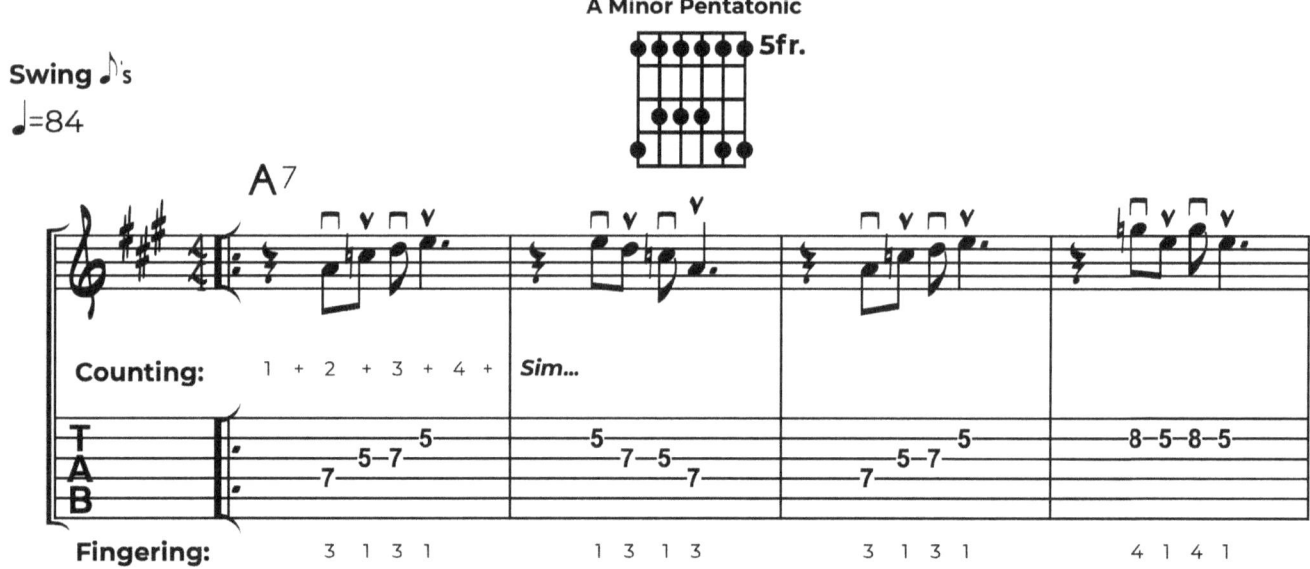

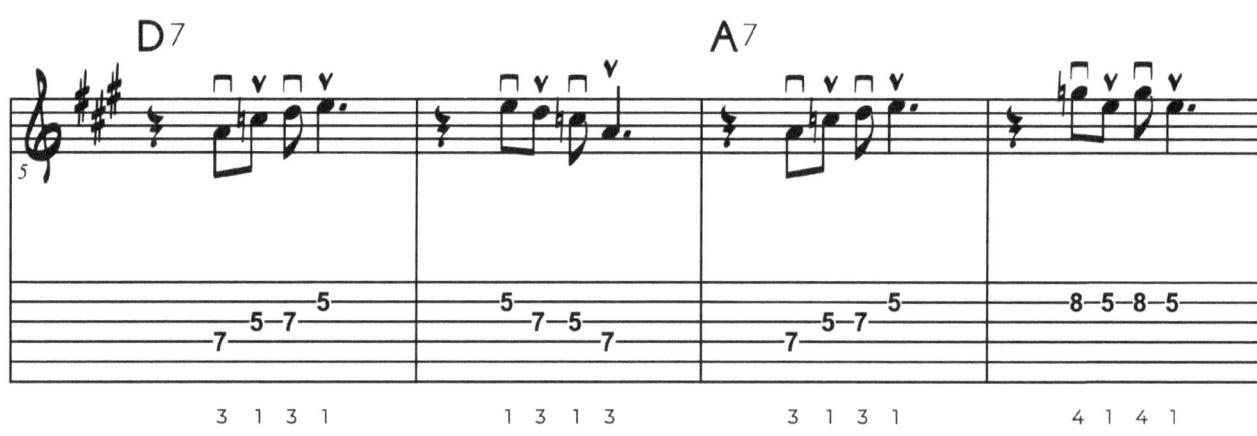

STRUMMING BLUES IN A

This strumming Blues in A is a simple but effective song that gives you a classic Blues sound while strumming the open A7, D7, and E7 chords. The rhythm will use 4 downstroke quarter notes per measure and although the strum pattern is easy it is important to lock into a groove to make it sound authentic. You can try accenting beats 2 and 4 by strumming a little harder on those beats.

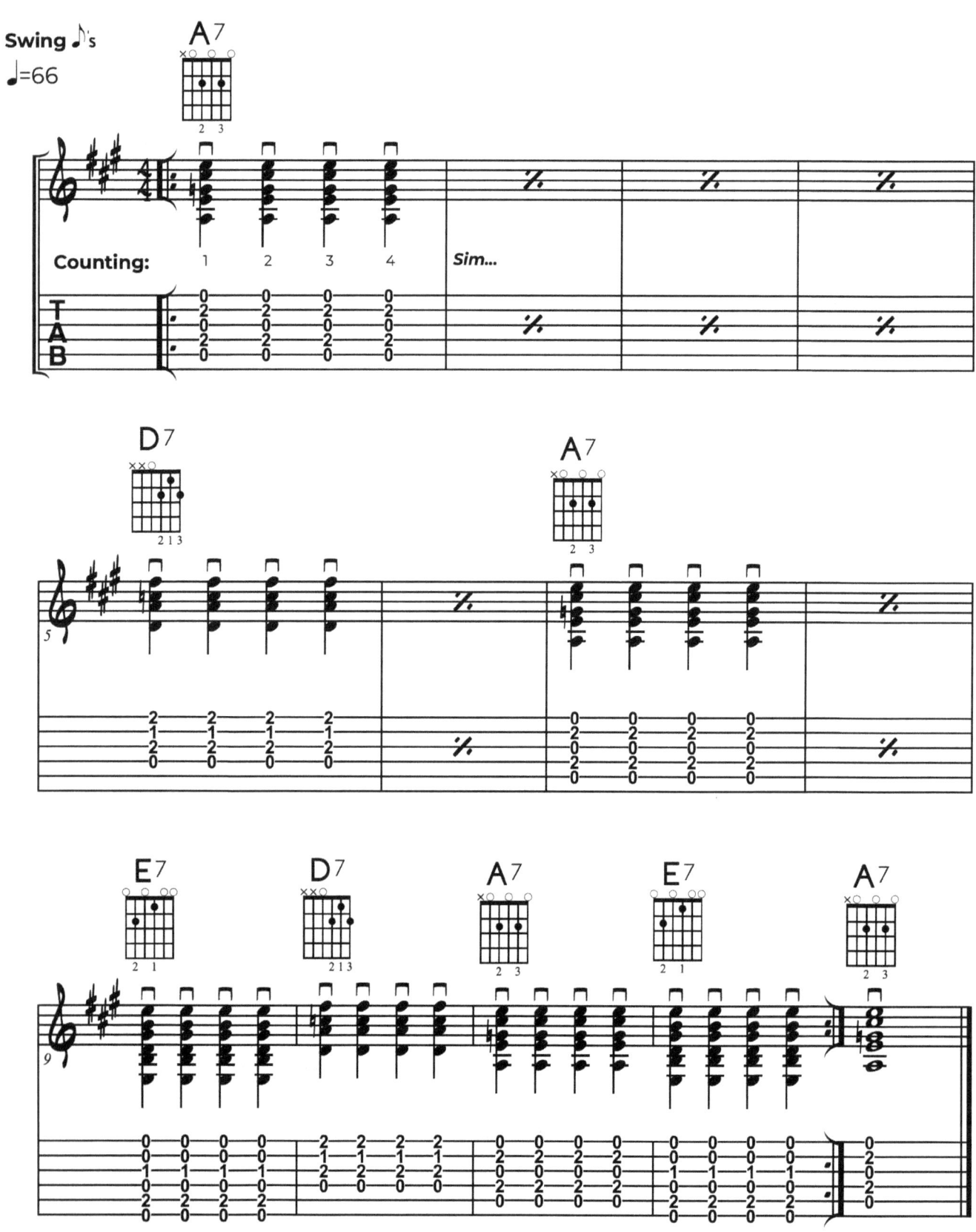

FINGERSTYLE BLUES - COUNTRY STROLLING

This Blues in "A" is played fingerstyle using a forward roll (lower to higher strings). The fingerstyle pattern is called the P.I.M.A pattern - thumb (p), index (i), middle (m), and ring (a) fingers, and one of the most widely used fingerstyle patterns in music. This will be played using straight 1/8th notes to give it an even and consistent feel.

BLUES SHUFFLE IN A *VARIATION #2*

Blues Variation #2 is based on Blues Variation #1, but it adds the G note (4th string, 5th fret) on beat 3 using your fourth finger. Typically, our fourth finger is the weakest of all our fingers, but with practice it will build up strength. Once you get this variation #2 down, you can start mixing both variation #1 and #2 in your playing. Use all downstrokes.

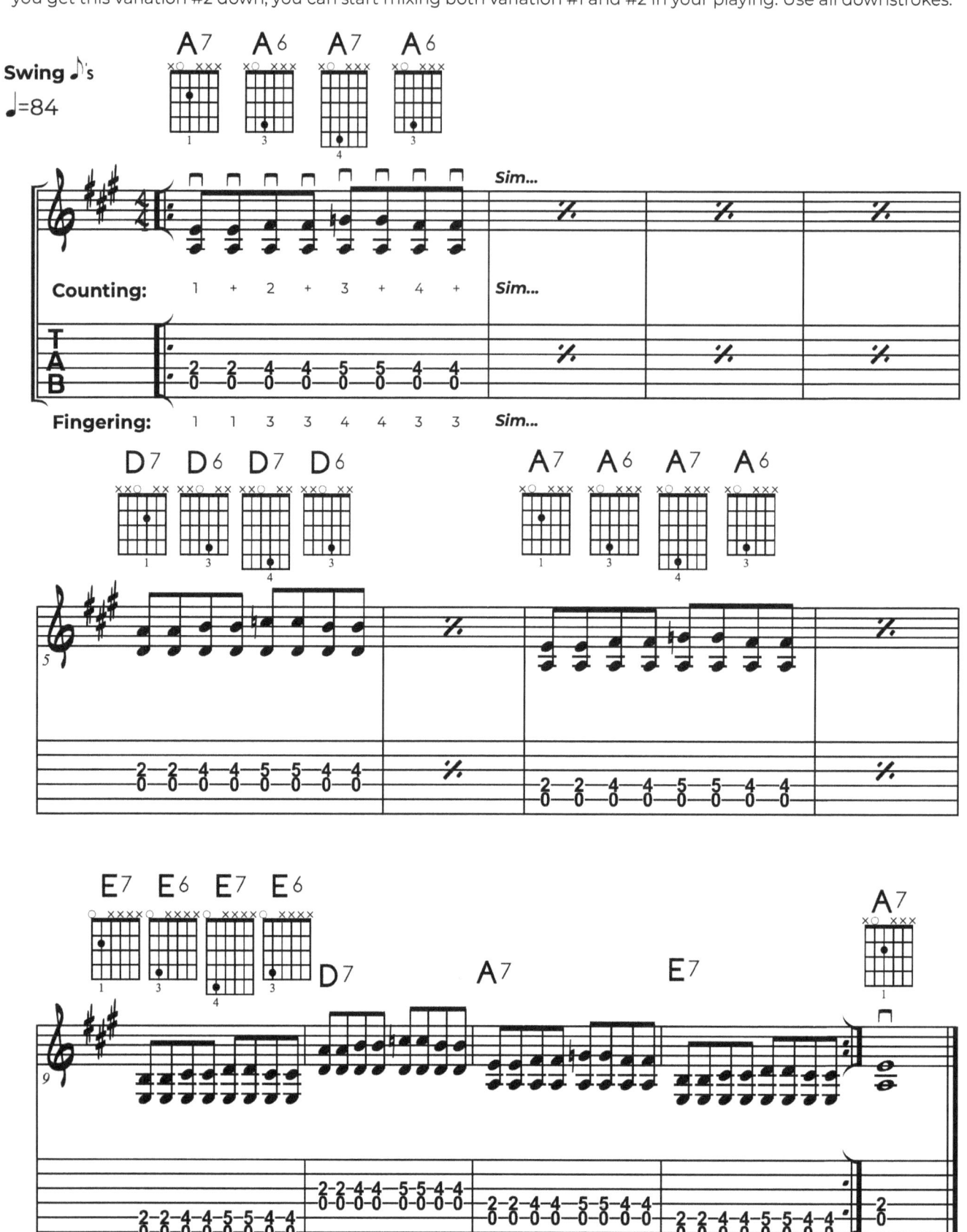

GOLD RUSH BLUES SOLO

This awesome solo works great over the Blues Shuffle in "A" and the notes come right from the "A" Blues scale. The Blues scale adds the "blue note" which is the Eb note (6th fret, 5th string and 8th fret, 3rd string). It may not seem like much, but this one "blue note" can make all the difference in creating a powerful Blues solo.

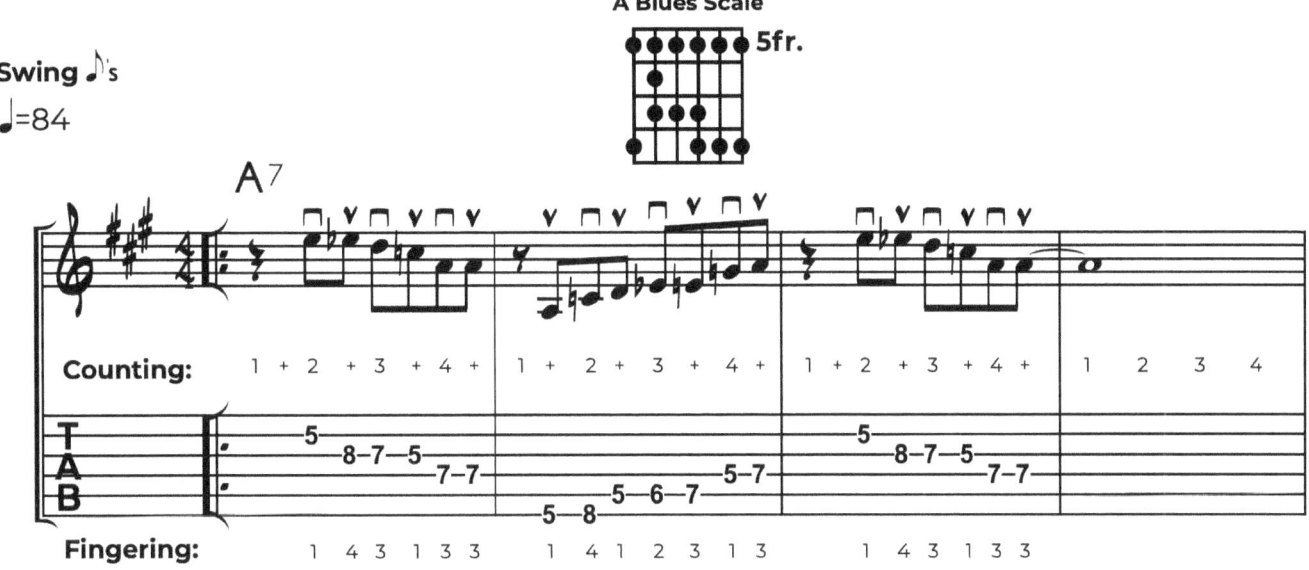

OCTAVE JUMP BLUES IN A

This variation of our Blues in "A" is based on a repeating pattern that starts off with an "Octave" jump. An "Octave" is 2 notes of the same pitch (in this case "A") that are eight diatonic notes apart, simply meaning that the notes sound the same, but one is an octave higher in pitch then the other. Notice that this Blues is in the closed position (no open strings) and starts on the 5th fret. Follow the fingerings and use alternate picking throughout.

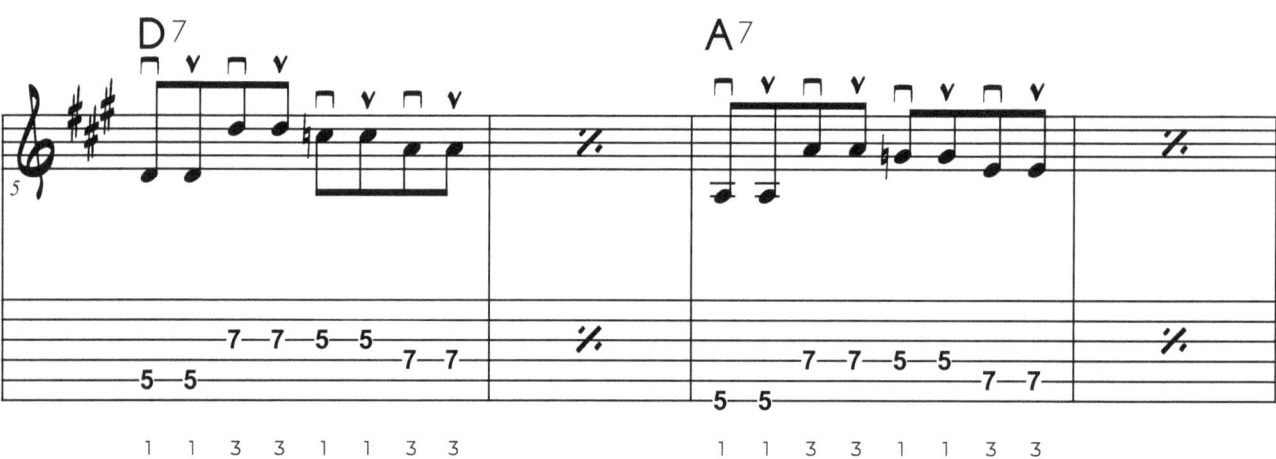

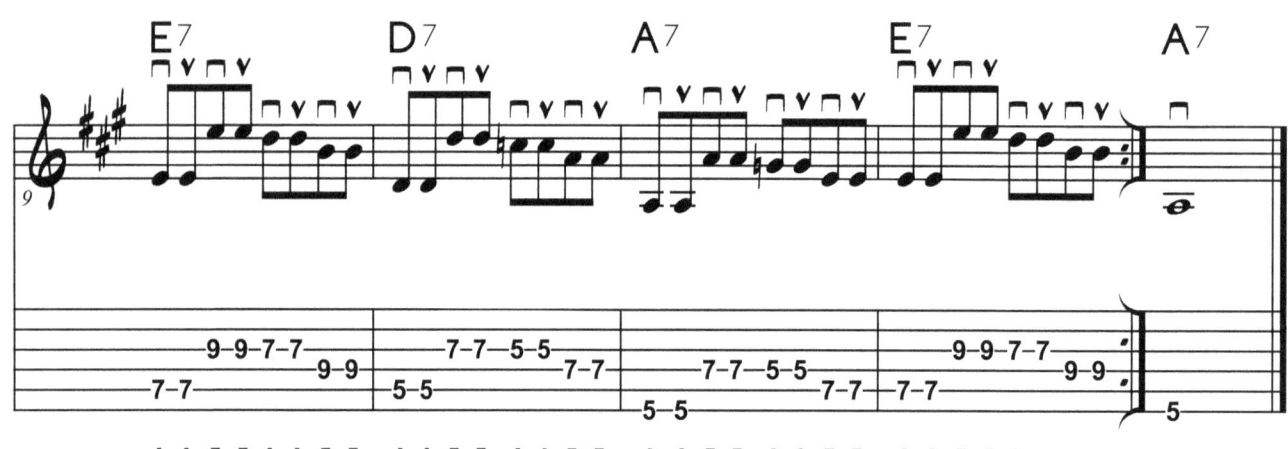

BLUES SHUFFLE IN A *VARIATION #3*

Third time is a charm and this one will blow your mind. This Blues variation is similar to variation #1 & #2 except it adds a single note "walking" bass sound on beats "2" and the "and of beat 2." The last measure adds a ½ step slide turnaround that goes from the F7 to the E7. This simple ½ step slide adds a bit of class and excitement to your Blues playing.

GREASY BLUES IN E *PG. 1 of 2*

This "Greasy" Blues in "E" uses a funky strum pattern followed by single notes. The key of E provides such cool open string licks that you hear in the greats like Stevie Ray Vaughan. The "x" on beat "2" of each measure is a "muted" strum. To get the "muted" sound place the palm of your strumming hand on the strings at the same time as you strum the strings with the pick. This funky Blues is played using straight 1/8th notes.

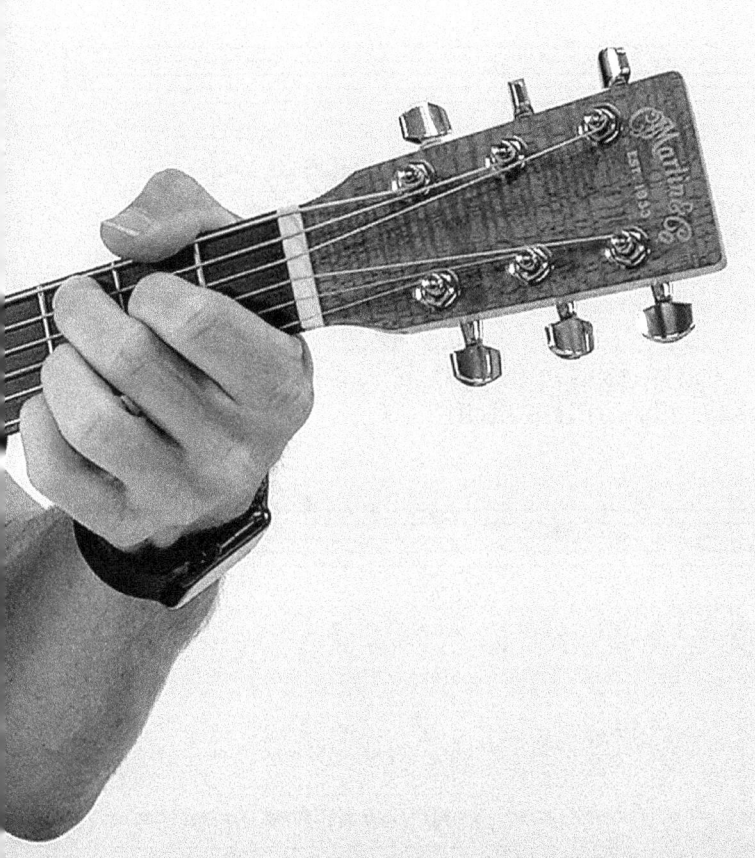

GREAT JOB!

I want to congratulate you for finishing the Rock Like The Pros Blues Guitar Mastery book by Terry Carter. You have been challenged, you've learned a lot in this book, and you should now have a better understanding of the Blues, be a better rhythm and lead guitar player, play with better rhythm, have more confidence and technique, and be ready to play with others.

If you are interested in more guitar, we have additional guitar courses and content at rocklikethepros.com. If you want to rock the Blues on the ukulele check out the Blues ukulele courses at **ukelikethepros.com.**

THE ESSENTIALS

It is important to learn and memorize these terms and symbols because they not only apply to guitar but to all music.

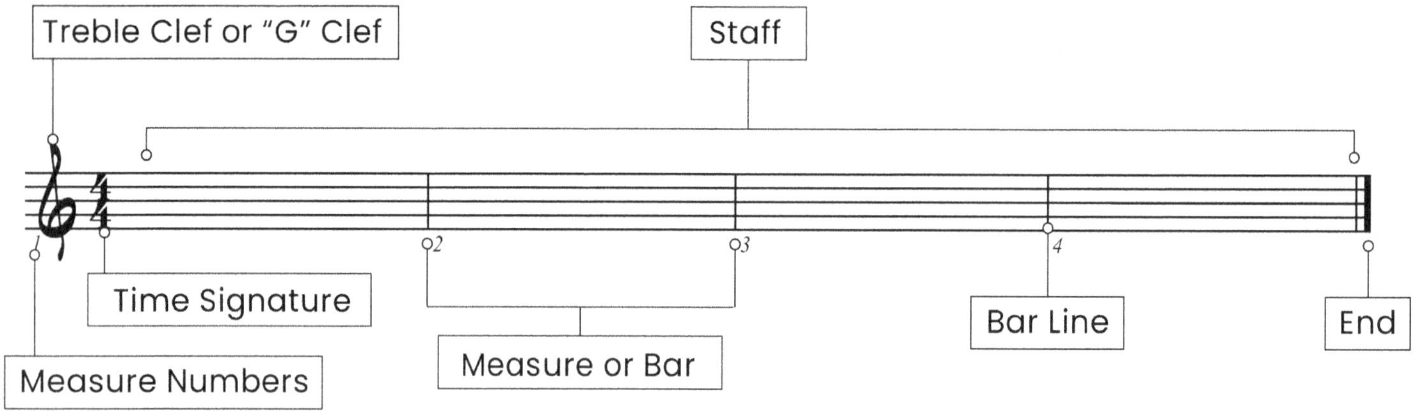

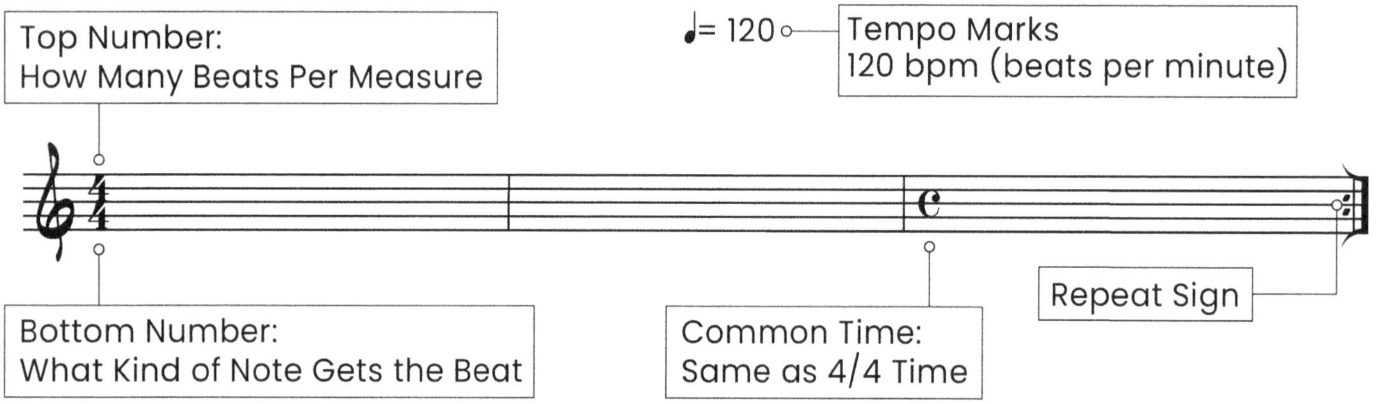

- Treble Clef or "G" Clef
- Staff
- Time Signature
- Measure Numbers
- Measure or Bar
- Bar Line
- End

- Top Number: How Many Beats Per Measure
- Tempo Marks: ♩= 120, 120 bpm (beats per minute)
- Bottom Number: What Kind of Note Gets the Beat
- Common Time: Same as 4/4 Time
- Repeat Sign

Notes On The Staff: There are seven notes in music (A, B, C, D, E, F, G) and they move up and down alphabetically on the staff.

E F G A B C D E F G A B C D E F G A B C

How To Remember The Notes:

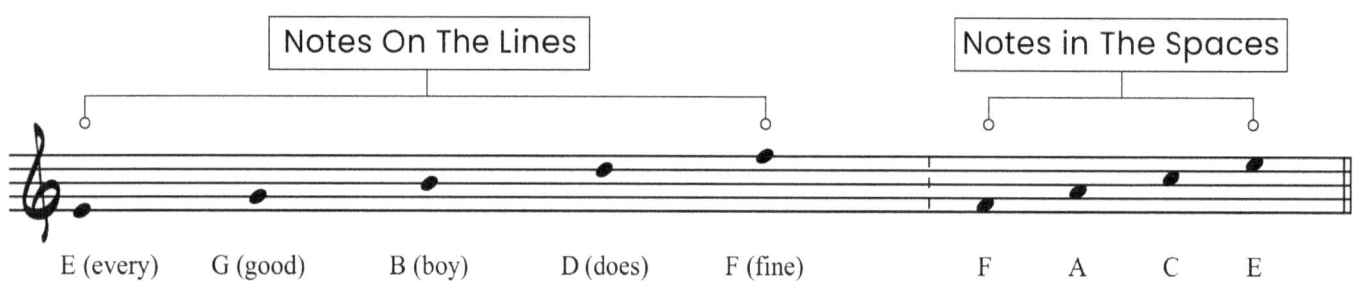

Notes On The Lines: E (every) G (good) B (boy) D (does) F (fine)

Notes in The Spaces: F A C E

A

HOW TO READ TAB

Tablature (TAB) is a form of music reading for guitar that uses a 6 line staff and numbers. Each line of the staff represents a string on the guitar and the numbers represent which fret you play on. When looking at the TAB staff it reads like it's upside down on the paper compared to the strings of your guitar. On the TAB staff, the highest line represents the 1st string (E string) of the guitar, while the lowest line represents the 6th string (E string) of the guitar. When you see 2 or more notes stacked on top of each other on the TAB staff, that means you play those notes at the same time, like a a chord.

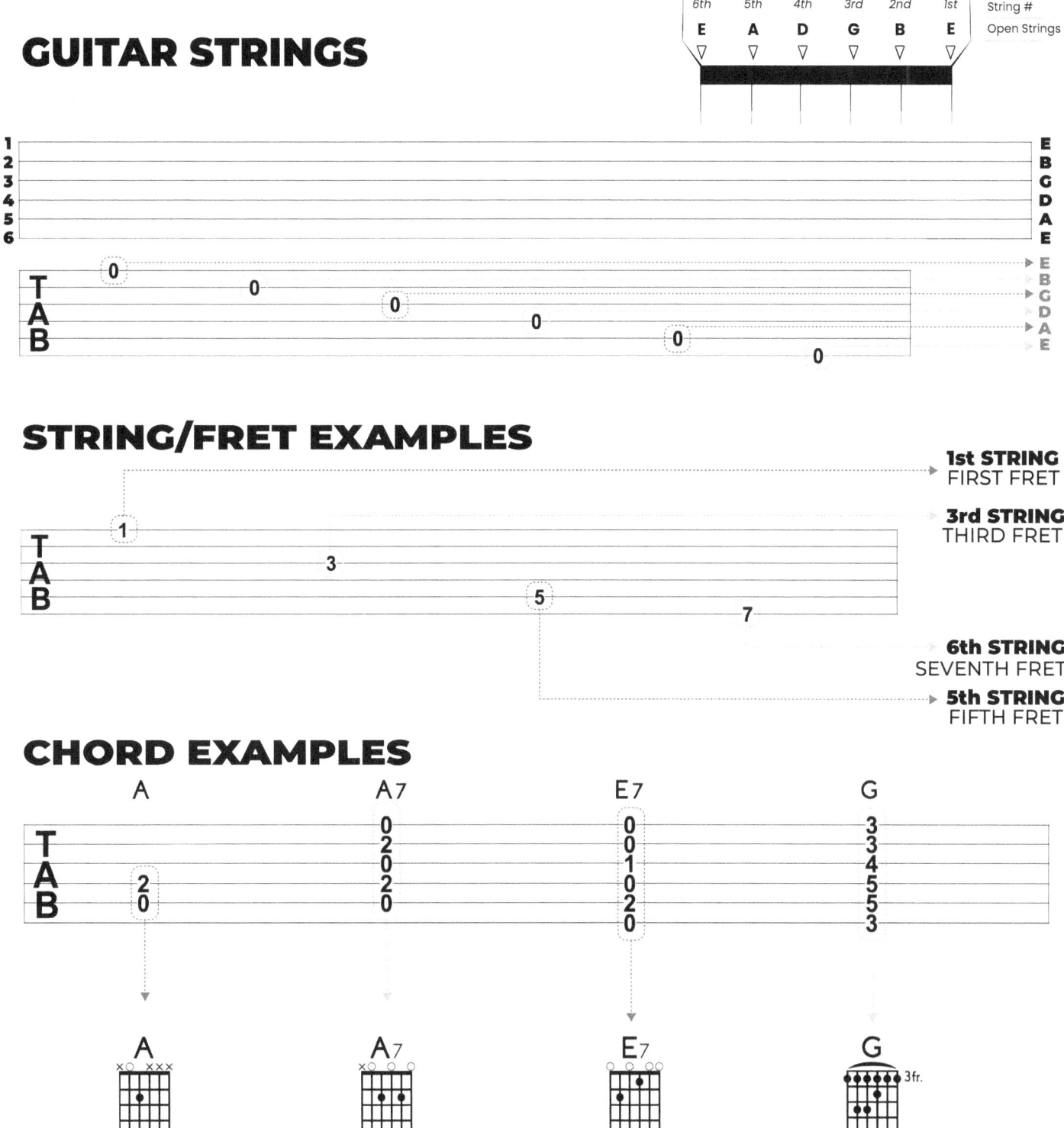

GUITAR PARTS

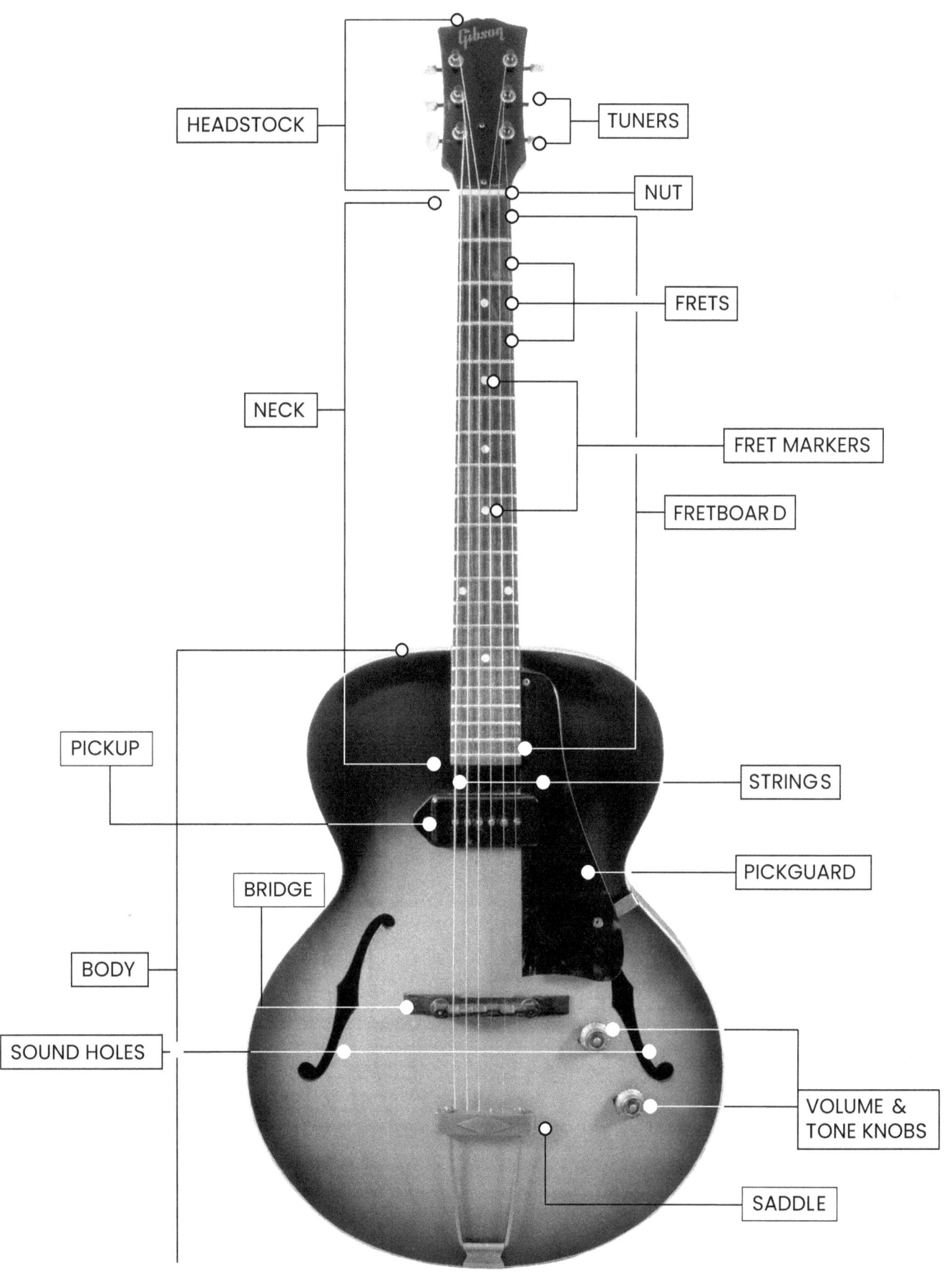

GUITAR HANDS

When playing fingerstyle on your guitar, you will see both letters and numbers to indicate which fingers to use both for picking hand and your fretting hand. These letters and numbers will show up in the music notation, TAB, and/or chord diagrams.

FRETTING HAND	PICKING HAND
The left hand for right-handed players, will be indicated in the music or chord diagrams by numbers: **1**=Index finger **3**=Ring finger **2**=Middle finger **4**=Pinky finger	The right hand for right-handed players, will be indicated in the music by letters: **p**=Thumb **m**=middle **i**=index **a**=ring **c**=pinky (not used in this course)

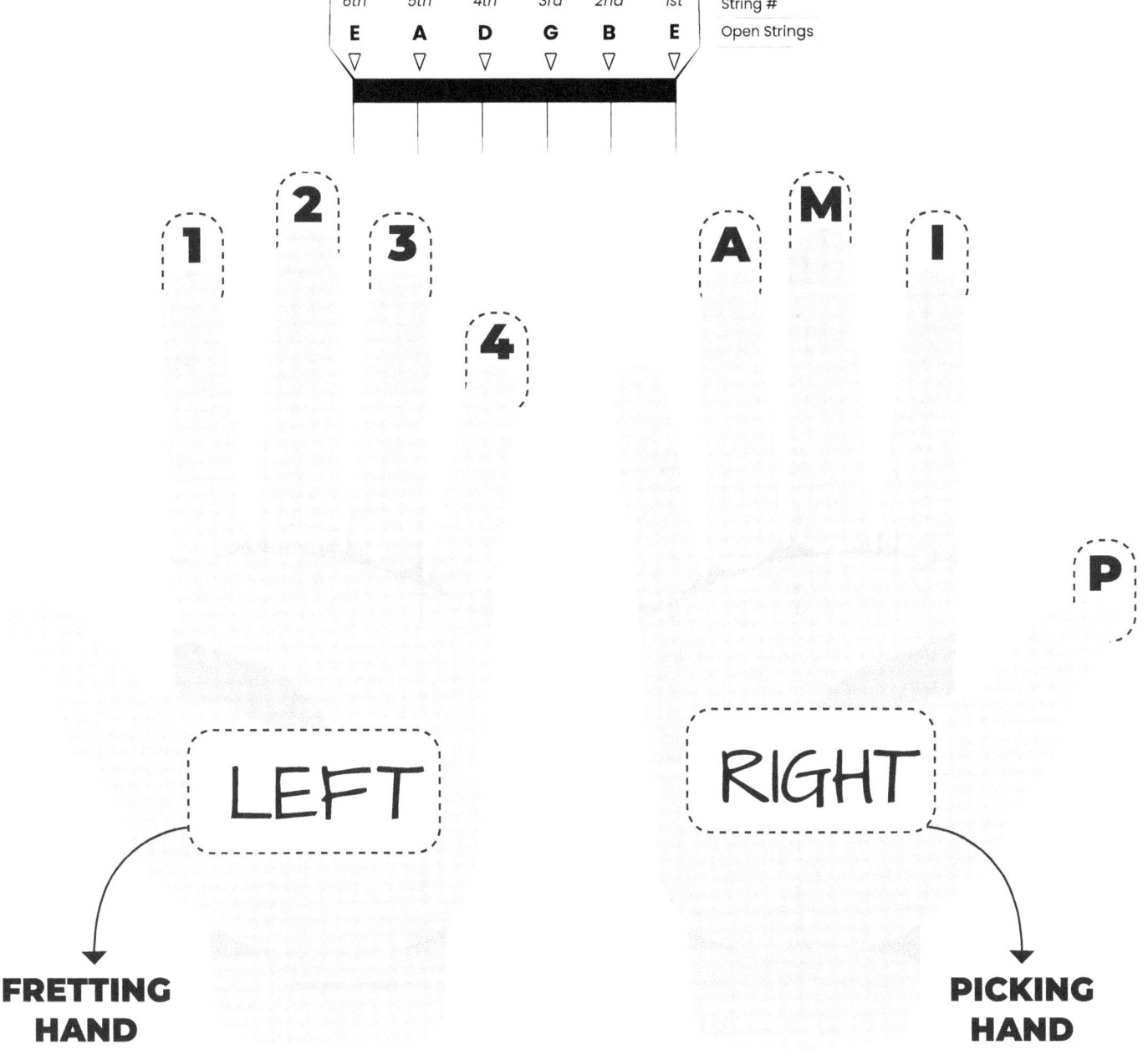

LEFT → FRETTING HAND

RIGHT → PICKING HAND

D

NOTES ON THE GUITAR NECK

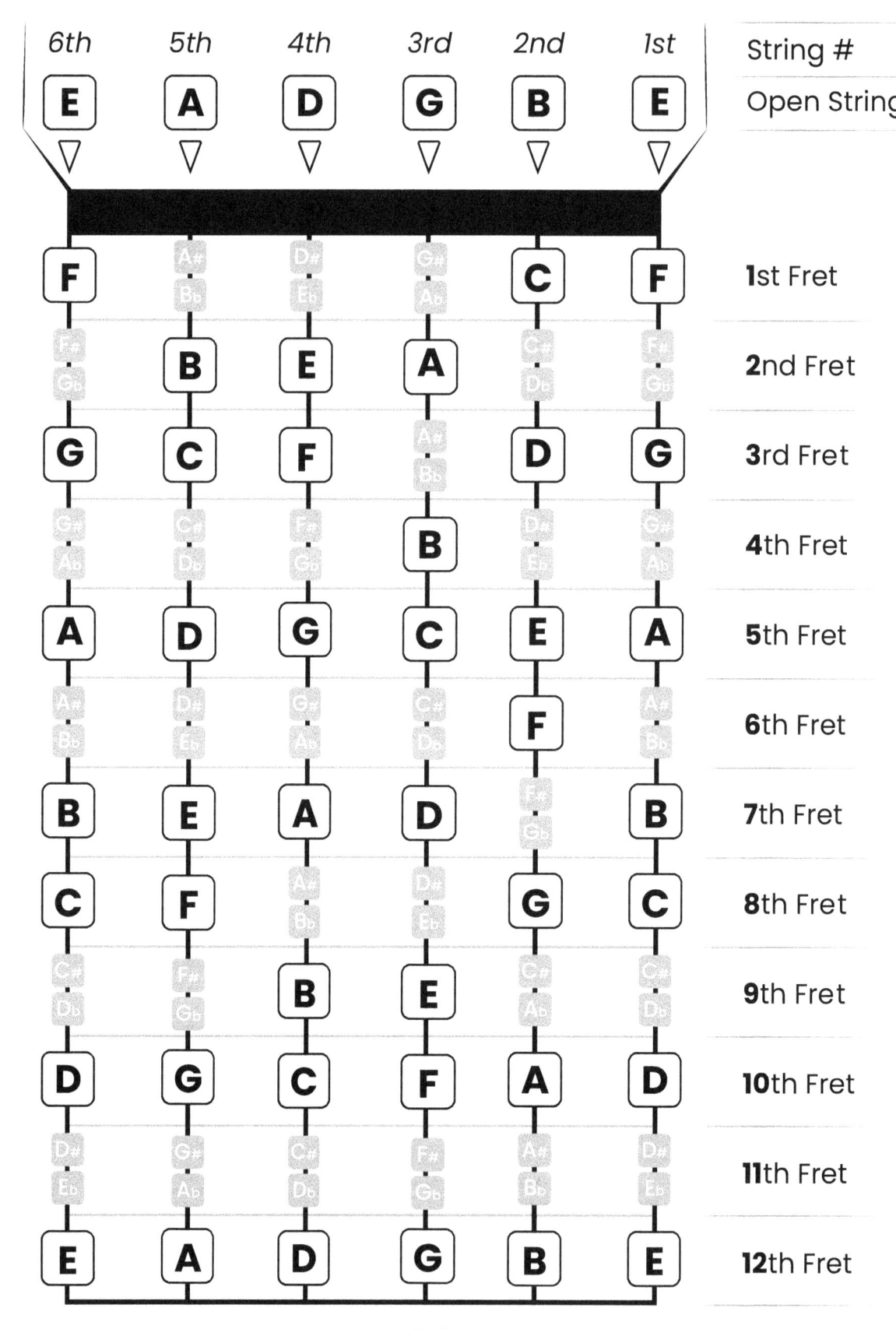

Notes repeat at 12th Fret

UNDERSTANDING CHORD DIAGRAMS

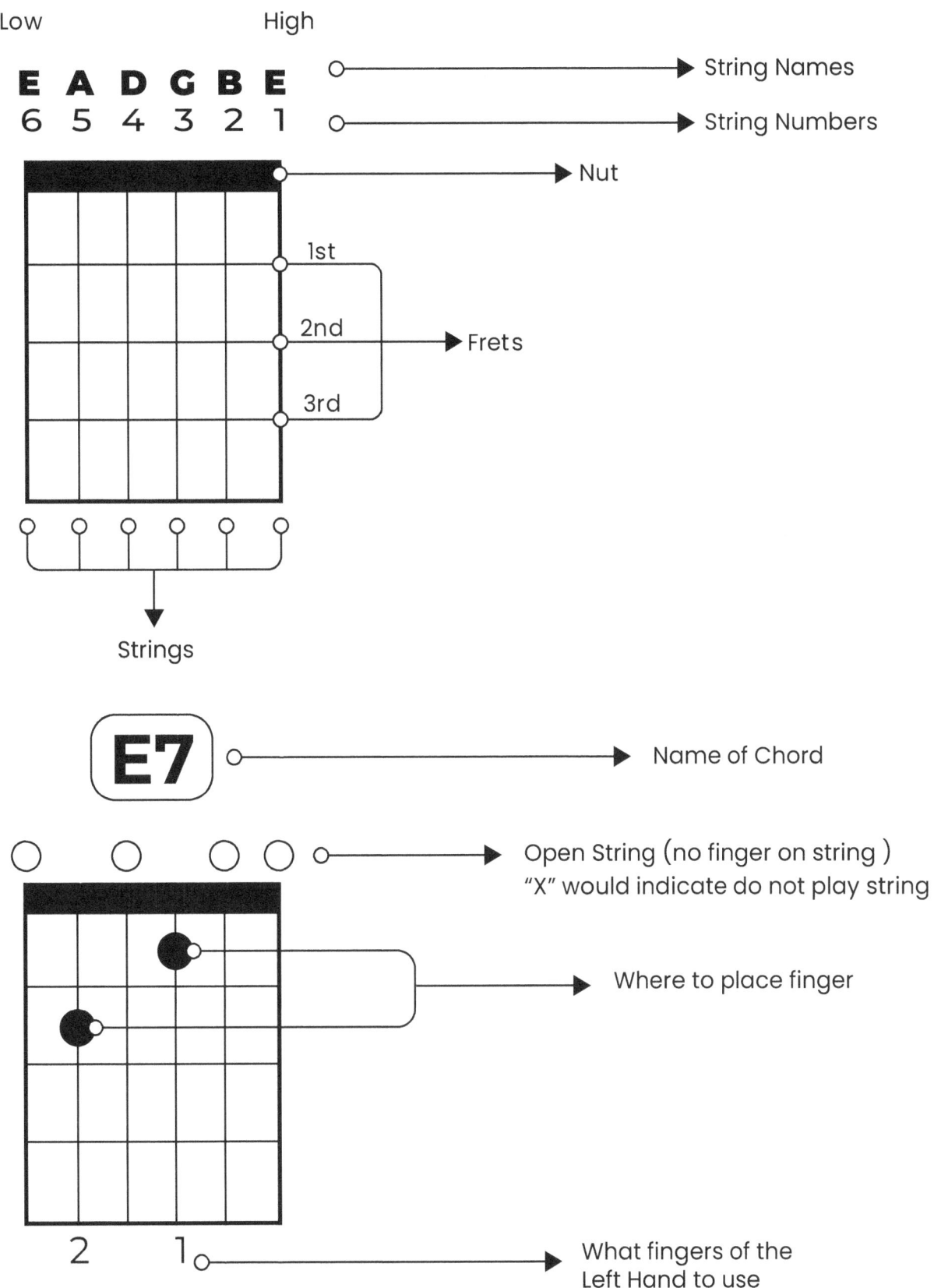

MUSIC SYMBOLS TO KNOW

A variety of symbols, articulations, repeats, hammer on's, pull off's, bends, and slides.

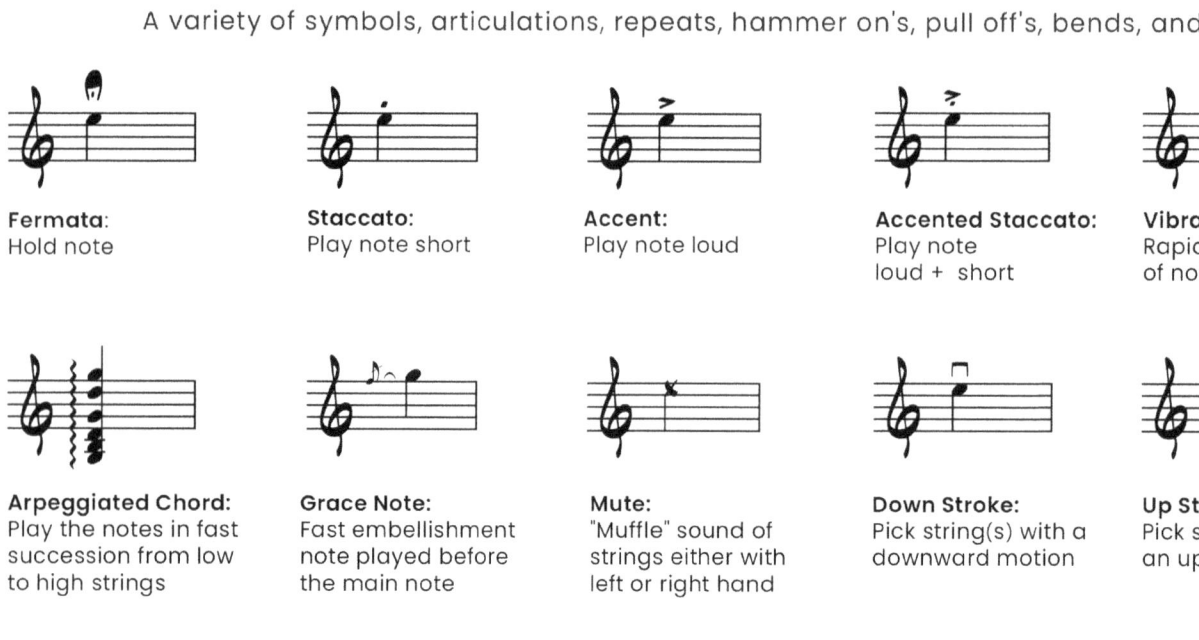

Fermata: Hold note

Staccato: Play note short

Accent: Play note loud

Accented Staccato: Play note loud + short

Vibrato: Rapid "shaking" of note

Arpeggiated Chord: Play the notes in fast succession from low to high strings

Grace Note: Fast embellishment note played before the main note

Mute: "Muffle" sound of strings either with left or right hand

Down Stroke: Pick string(s) with a downward motion

Up Stroke: Pick string(s) with an upward motion

Tie: Play first note but do not play second note that it is tied to

Ledger Lines: Extend the staff higher or lower.

Slash Notation: Repeat notes & rhythms from previous measure

1 Bar Repeat: Repeat notes & rhythms from previous measure

2 Bar Repeat: Repeat notes & rhythms from previous 2 measures

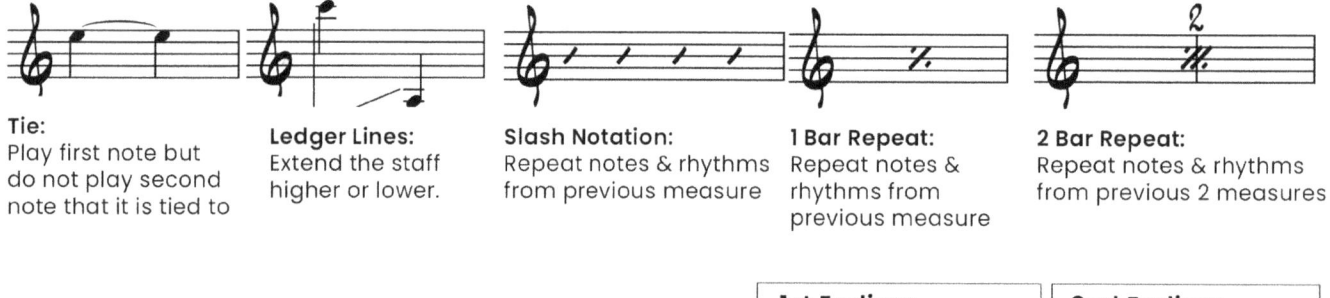

Repeat Sign: (Beginning)

Repeat Sign: (End)

1st Ending: Play this part the first time only

2nd Ending: Play this part the second time

(D.C. AL FINE) — *D.C.* (da capo) means go to the beginning of the tune and stop when you get to *Fine*

(D.C. AL CODA) — *D.C.* means go to the beginning of the tune and jump to *Coda* ⊕ when you see the sign ⊕

(D.S. AL FINE) — *D.S.* (dal segno) means go to the *Sign* 𝄋 and stop when you get to *Fine*

(D.S. AL CODA) — *D.S.* means go to the *Sign* 𝄋 And Jump to the *Coda* ⊕ when you see ⊕

SIM… — Play the same rhythm, strum pattern, or picking pattern as the previous measure

ETC… — Continue the same rhythm, strum pattern, or picking pattern as the previous measure

Hammer On:
Pick first note then hammer on to the next note without picking it.

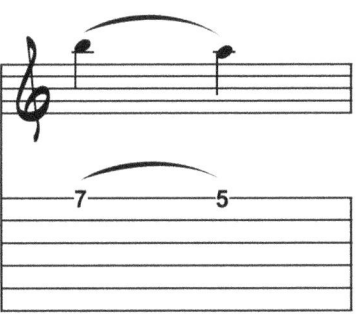

Pull Off:
Pick first note then pull off to the next note without picking it.

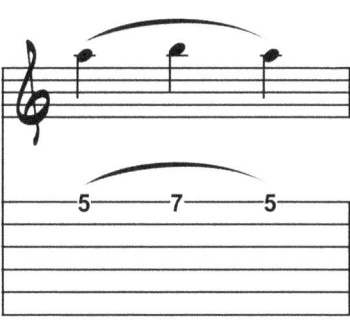

Hammer On & Pull Off:
Pick first note, hammer on to the next note, and pull off to the last note all in one motion.

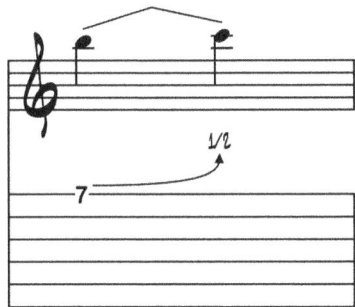

1/2 Step Bend:
Bend the first note a 1/2 step or 1 fret.

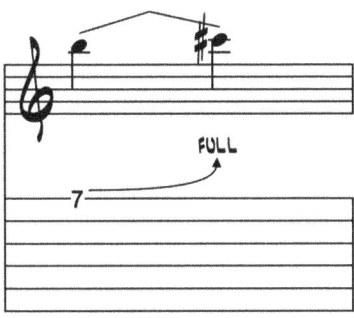

Whole Step Bend:
Bend the first note a whole step or 2 frets.

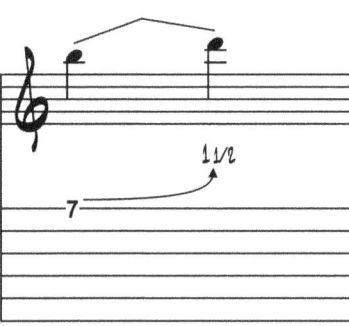

Step & 1/2 Bend:
Bend the first note 1 1/2 steps or 3 frets

Forward Slide:
Pick first note and slide up to higher note.

Backward Slide:
Pick first note and slide back to lower note.

Forward/Backward Slide:
Pick first note, slide up to next note and then slide back.

Slide Into Note:
Slide from 2-3 frets below note

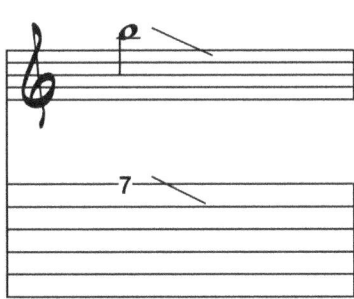

Slide Off Note:
Slide off 2-5 frets after note

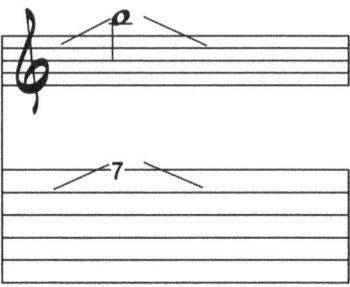

Slide Into Note then Slide Off Note

GUITAR CHORD CHART

These are some of the most widely used chords in all of music. Although there are more chords than what is listed, these chords represent the most widely used shapes.
The string names (from high to low) are:

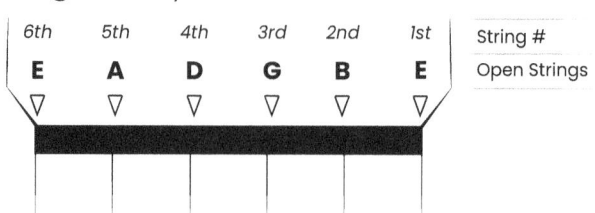

MAJOR CHORDS

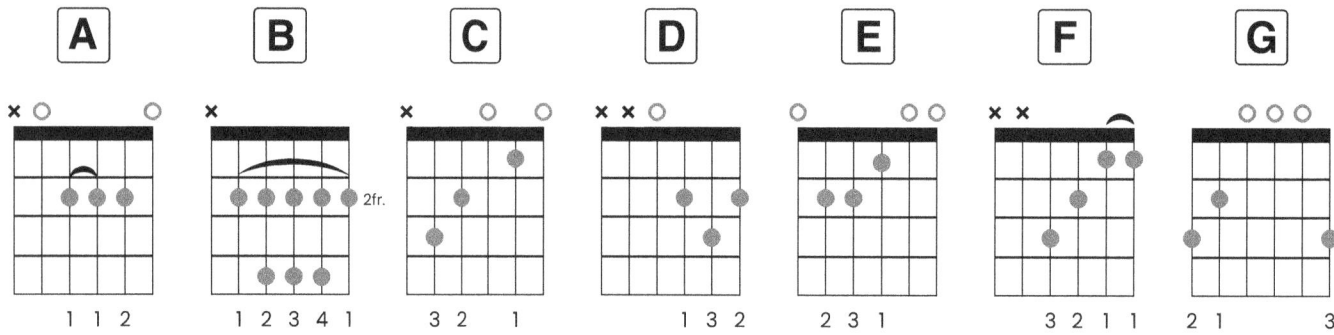

MINOR CHORDS

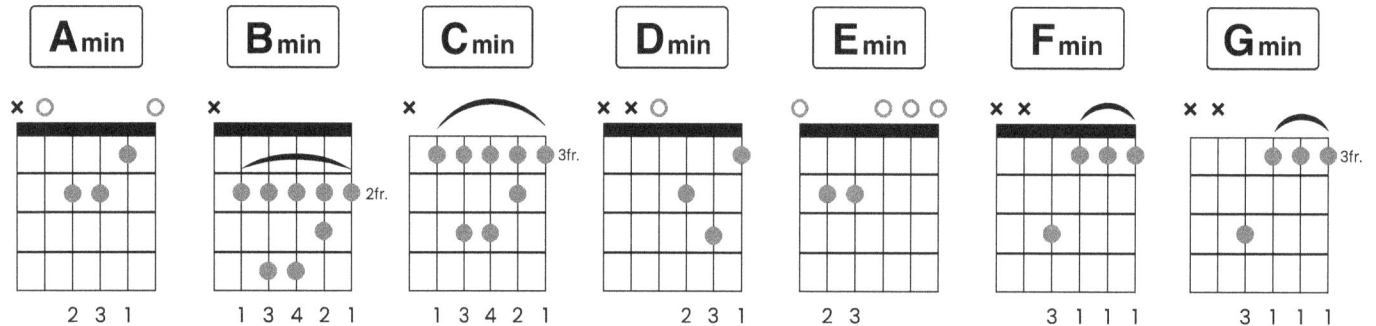

DOMINANT 7th CHORDS

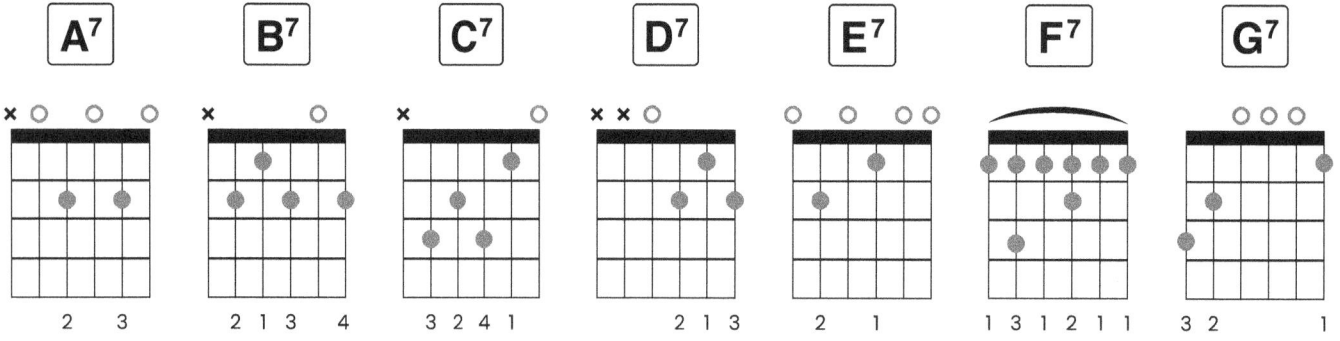

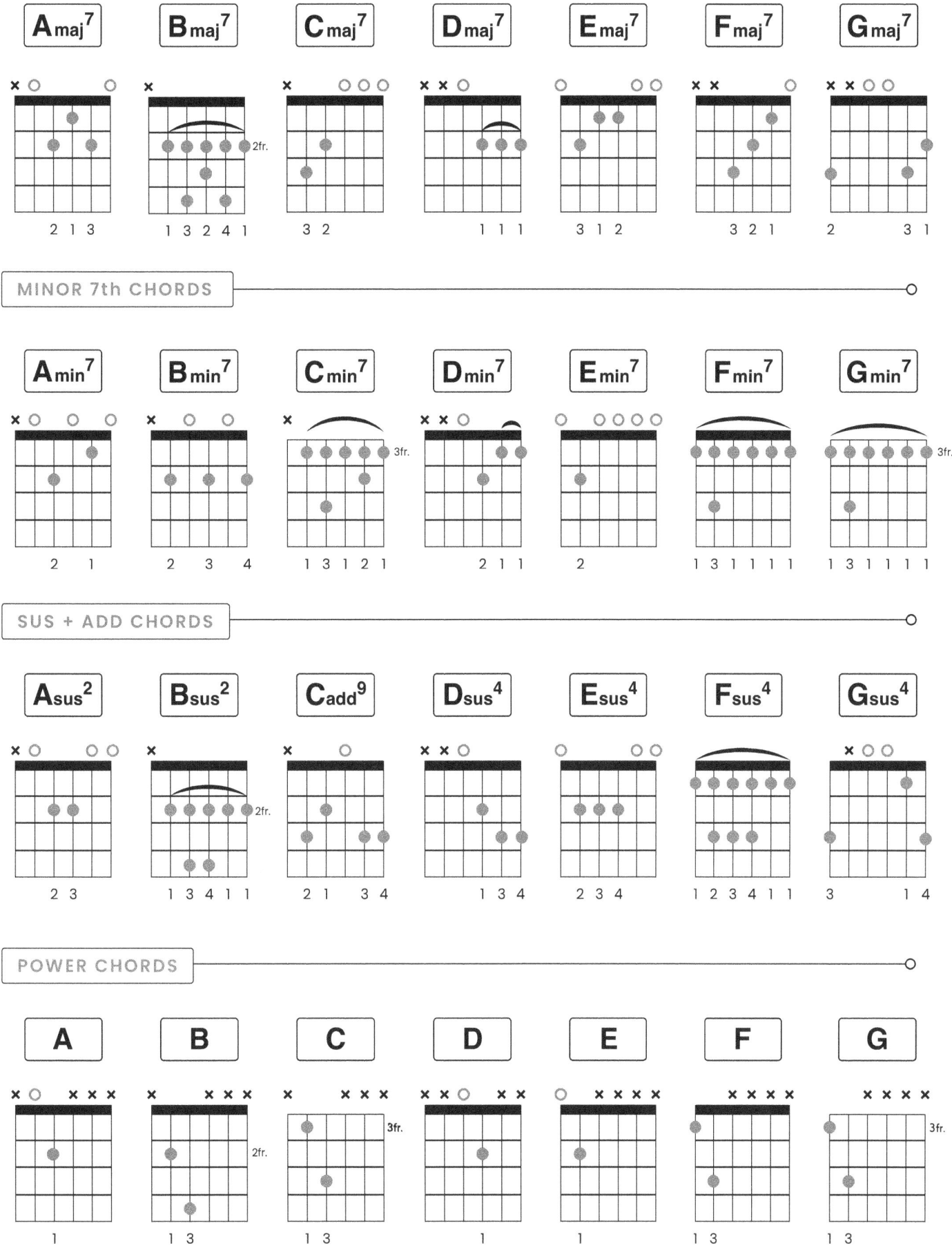

BASIC RHYTHMS

The 3 main rhythms in this lesson are whole notes, half notes and quarter notes.

ESSENTIAL RHYTHMS

The 4 main rhythms in this lesson are whole notes, half notes, quarter notes and eighth notes.

ABOUT THE AUTHOR

Terry Carter is a San Diego-based guitar and ukulele player, surfer, songwriter, and creator of rocklikethepros.com, ukelikethepros.com, and terrycartermusicstore.com.

With over 25 years as a professional musician, educator and Los Angeles studio musician, Terry has worked with greats like Weezer, Josh Groban, Robby Krieger (The Doors), 2-time Grammy winning composer Christopher Tin (Calling All Dawns), Duff McKagan (Guns N' Roses), Grammy winning producer Charles Goodan (Santana/Rolling Stones), and the Los Angeles Philharmonic.

Terry has written and produced tracks for commercials (Discount Tire and Puma) and TV shows, including Scorpion (CBS), Pit Bulls & Parolees (Animal Planet), Trippin', Wildboyz, and The Real World (MTV). He has self-published over 25 books for Uke Like The Pros and Rock Like The Pros, filmed over 30 ukulele and guitar online courses, and has tens of millions of views on his docial media channels. Terry received a Master of Music in Studio/Jazz Guitar Performance from University of Southern California and a Bachelor of Music from San Diego State University, with an emphasis in Jazz Studies and Music Education. He has taught at the University of Southern California, San Diego State University, Santa Monica College, Miracosta College, and Los Angeles Trade Tech College.

TERRY CARTER MUSIC STORE
All your music needs at the #1 music store, **terrycartermusicstore.com**

Guitars

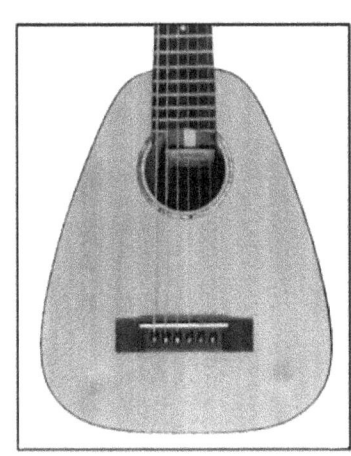

Guitarleles

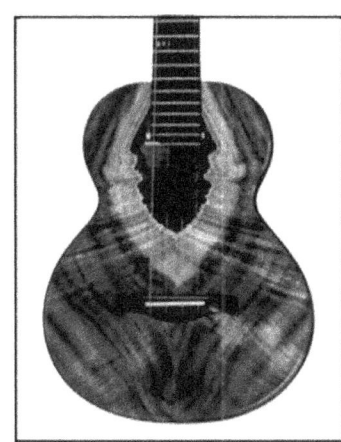

Ukuleles

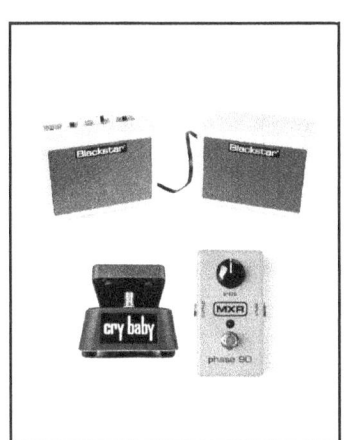

Amplifiers and Pedals

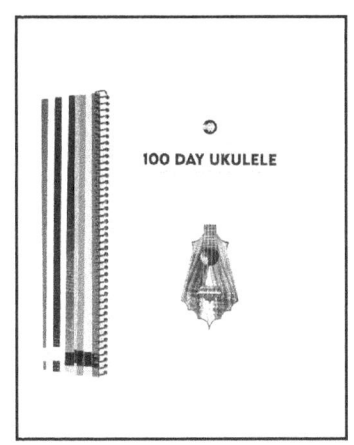

Books

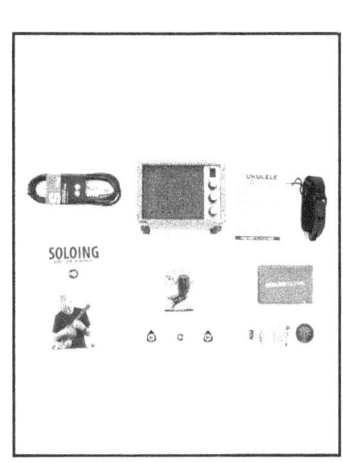

Accessories

ONLINE GUITAR COURSES
The perfect place to learn how to play and master the guitar.

BEGINNER COURSES

GUITAR STARTER COURSE

EASY & ESSENTIAL **STRUM PATTERNS** COURSE

PRACTICE & TECHNIQUE BOOTCAMP

BEGINNING **STRUMMING MASTERY** COURSE

BEGINNING **MUSIC READING** COURSE

BEGINNING **BLUES MASTERY** COURSE

INTERMEDIATE COURSES

INTERNMEDIATE **STRUMMING MASTERY** COURSE

INTERMEDIATE **MUSIC READING** COURSE

INTERMEDIATE **BLUES MASTERY** COURSE

ADVANCED COURSES

20 IMPORTANT **STRUM PATTERNS**

ADVANCED **STRUMMING** MASTERY

Courses For All Levels
ROCKLIKETHEPROS.COM

ROCKLIKETHEPROS.COM
UKELIKETHEPROS.COM
BLOG.UKELIKETHEPROS.COM
TERRYCARTERMUSICSTORE.COM
BUYSTRINGSONLINE.COM

@rocklikethepros

INTERESTED IN UKULELE CONTENT?
UKELIKETHEPROS.COM

www.ingramcontent.com/pod-product-compliance
Lightning Source LLC
Chambersburg PA
CBHW081356040426
42451CB00017B/3476